A Letter...
from Jacqui

Katie has worked extremely hard to make this book a success and I am sure that you will have a great treat in store! George and Freddie have been busy helping their mum to prepare numerous delicious dishes to produce this book. I have been very tempted by the photographs I have seen at George's hospital appointments!

This book is a fundraising activity for children with lymphoedema. With the help of Katie and her family and friends, we have already made great advances in improving the situation for children and their families and a book for children with lymphoedema is now ready to be published and will be available for hospitals and doctors in both this country and overseas. Thank you for supporting this initiative and helping us to address some of the problems that face young people with lymphoedema.

My very best wishes and thanks

Jacquelyn C Todd

Dr Jacquelyne Todd

Physiotherapist Consultant in Lymphoedema

A Note...
from Katie

As a child, I was a fussy eater and it horrifies me now! That's not to say that Mum didn't encourage me to eat healthily because she did ... I guess I was just stubborn and things haven't changed much!

However, I took a very keen interest in 'Home Economics' at school, mainly for the entertainment value, and although I was still fussy with my food, it gave me a great insight into cooking. I took great pleasure in helping with the cooking at home, especially reeling in the praise received from dinner party guests when my parents were entertaining.

From learning about food and playing around with it, creating interesting and tasty dishes, I soon became a bit of a 'foodie' and haven't looked back since!

Recently, two great friends of mine (Tamara and Lindsay) put pressure on me to write a book and I insisted it would be impossible because I'm a 'chuck-it-in' type of cook. I stressed that I never weigh, measure or time a recipe and it would be difficult for me to put pen to paper and pass on some of my recipes.

Not long after that late evening, putting the world to rights, I awoke one morning at 3am with a huge incentive to write a book ... totally bizarre! And the worst of it was that the name of the book was also there, at that ridiculous time of night! I planned and plotted and by 'proper' morning I was suddenly on another mission. It all made sense ... my youngest son, George, suffers with primary lymphoedema; he follows a healthy diet and also loves cooking. No microwave in our house!

Some of the recipes may look complicated but I can assure you that they are all very easy! They should suit children and adults alike and if you have fussy kids then I hope they can learn and take pleasure with helping in the kitchen, just as I did. From encouraging your children to learn about food, how to prepare it and be creative in the kitchen, they will hopefully learn to enjoy the delights of flavours, textures, smells and presentation.

Sadly, many schools do not encourage this talent and it is left to the parents to promote it in the home ... so, go for it and give your youngsters the basis of a good appreciation of food to take them through life ... a social skill, no less!

Make your children aware of sourcing good food ... home produce can be fairly easy and is certainly worth a try! Enquire about your local farmers markets and farm shops and help support your local producers, butchers, fishmongers, bakers, etc. So much pleasure can be had by letting your little ones get involved in picking their own fruit and vegetables, choosing their own produce from a market and, of course, getting their hands dirty in the garden is bound to be fun!

To give you maybe twice as many recipes as most children's cookery books, I haven't gone into graphic detail for the recipes as I hope, like myself, that you wouldn't let your child loose in the kitchen with hot ovens, boiling water and sharp knives until you are totally confident with their capabilities. Common sense, of course! Once you've guided them in the right direction and even made a recipe once together then I am certain they will willingly repeat the recipe on their own the next time ... my own children have their favourite dishes they like to make and I'm thrown out of the kitchen by eagerness taking over!

I hope you find much enjoyment on your journey through this book and I thank you for supporting the Leeds Lymphoedema Service and the Leeds Teaching Hospitals.

Much love

Katie Taylor
x

By George...
It's Scrummy

About this book

With over 100 recipes and ideas, this book has been produced to raise awareness and vital funds for advancing knowledge and research into lymphoedema. Every copy sold will enable the Leeds Teaching Hospitals to help children, like George, who suffer with this debilitating condition.

What is Lymphoedema?

Lymphoedema is caused when the lymph system is unable to drain fluid away from the tissues, commonly causing swelling in limbs and can increase the risk of infection. It can affect anyone at any age and can affect any part of the body.

Lymphoedema can be painful. Although the condition cannot be cured, with the appropriate treatment it can be improved and controlled. Treatment is vital, as leaving it untreated will result in deterioration.

There are two types of lymphoedema; primary and secondary. Primary lymphoedema is usually determined from birth and may be due to underdevelopment of the lymphatic system. It can affect infants, children or adults at any age.

Secondary lymphoedema can occur in the treatment of cancer following surgery or radiotherapy. It can also occur as a result of infection, severe injury, burns or any other trauma.

Understanding the condition and receiving information and advice on how to adapt to everyday living are key elements to a patient's successful management of lymphoedema.

Recipes...
By Season

Contents

Spring

Summer

Summer BBQ

Autumn

Winter

Conversions
Table

Oven Temperatures		
Mark 1	275°F	140°C
2	300	150
3	325	170
4	350	180
5	375	190
6	400	200
7	425	220
8	450	230
9	475	240

Measurements	
1/8 inch	3 mm
1/4	5 mm
1/2	1 cm
3/4	2
1	2.5
1 1/4	3
1 1/2	4
1 3/4	4.5
2	5
2 1/2	6
3	7.5
3 1/2	9
4	10
5	13
5 1/4	13.5
6	15
6 1/2	16
7	18
7 1/2	19
8	20
9	23
9 1/2	24
10	25.5
11	28
12	30

All these measurements are approximate conversions, which have either been rounded up or down.

Weights	
1/2 oz	10 g
3/4	20
1	25
1 1/2	40
2	50
2 1/2	60
3	75
4	110
4 1/2	125
5	150
6	175
7	200
8	225
9	250
10	275
12	350
1 lb	450
1 1/2	700
2	900
3	1.35 kg
3 1/2	1.55
4	1.80

Volume	
2 fl oz	55ml
3	75
5 (1/4 pt)	150
1/2 pt	275
3/4	425
1	570
1 1/4	725
1 3/4	1 litre
2	1.2
2 1/2	1.5
4	2.25

All about...
Carbohydrates

Carbohydrates such as cereals, bread, pasta, rice and potatoes are our main source of energy and health experts believe they should make up the bulk of our diet – roughly 50%.

Carbohydrates can be refined or unrefined. Refined carbohydrates include white bread, pasta and noodles made from white flour, white rice and sugary cereals. 'Refined' means that the bran and the germ have been removed from the grain, so the refined carbohydrates are lower in fibre.

Unrefined carbohydrates include wholemeal pasta, brown rice, wholemeal bread, porridge oats and other wholegrain cereals. These will provide more fibre and keep you feeling fuller for longer; also, wholegrain cereals can help maintain a healthy heart.

It's easy to swap staples such as pasta for the wholemeal version ... especially when served with a favourite sauce. They probably won't even notice the difference!

Potatoes, of course, are one of our staples and extremely versatile ... what could be an easier or healthier meal than a jacket potato served with beans or cheese for protein, with a salad? Surprisingly, spuds are also a good source of vitamin C.

Most children love potatoes in whatever form you choose to serve them, and for extra healthiness, try making chips or wedges in the oven, leaving the skins on.

Fruit...
and Vegetables

One of the best ways to ensure good health and vitality is to make sure we are getting our five portions a day of fruit and vegetables. This can seem a bit daunting ... especially when it comes to getting them into the children, and the old-fashioned 'meat and three veg' style dinners don't always appeal, especially during the summer months.

However, there are lots of different ways in which we can present vegetables that are so much more appealing than the boiled cabbage and sprouts we all remember from our childhoods.

Stir-fried vegetables are crunchy and keep their colour well ... the light cooking method retains the vitamin content, so it is healthier too. Chopped (or even minced for the very sensitive!) vegetables can be added to pasta sauces, and many children (and adults) prefer raw vegetables to be presented as finger foods for dipping into hummus, for example. Try chopping up carrots and peppers, or offering raw sugar snap peas or baby sweetcorn.

Children also love to prepare salads, and if they grow their own they are even more likely to eat them. Try sowing a packet of mixed salad seeds into a pot on the patio ... they are more or less fail-safe.

Smoothies are now more popular than ever, and can be a great way of getting fruit into children. However, juice and smoothies only count as one portion per day, no matter how much we drink.

A good rule to remember when it comes to fruit and veg is to 'eat a rainbow'. Differently coloured fruits and vegetables contain different vitamins and minerals, so eating from the whole spectrum will ensure that we are getting all the nutrients we need for good health, as well as plenty of fibre.

Herbs are an excellent way to give flavour to recipes without relying too much on salt. Again, they are very easy to grow and require little space ... a tub on the patio will do.

Of course, the very best fruit and vegetables are locally grown and seasonal ... they will have lost none of their flavour or nutritional value in transit. If you are lucky enough to have a farmer's market nearby, these can be an excellent source of local fruit and vegetables, and children may even be able to get involved with picking their own food. Involvement with the growing and cooking of fruit and vegetables can be one of the best ways to encourage children to eat them!

Dairy...
and Eggs

Eggs are a fantastic source of protein and their versatility makes them indispensable to any cook.

Egg dishes are usually quick and easy to make, and can have other ingredients added to make a more substantial meal ... try adding peas and peppers to an omelette, or some flaked smoked fish to scrambled eggs.

Eggs have come under fire recently for their high cholesterol level, but health experts now tell us that the cholesterol found in eggs is the 'good' kind and therefore not bad for our health.

Of course, the best eggs for flavour are free range; these are becoming more and more popular as people are starting to think more about where their food comes from.

Many farm shops have their own flocks of hens so that the customers can see for themselves the conditions in which their eggs are produced.

Dairy products are essential for healthy bones, teeth, muscles and nerves.

Milk, yoghurt and cheese are excellent sources of calcium and thankfully are popular with most children.

Eggs and milk are also an essential component of many recipes, including cakes and puddings, so if your child maintains that he or she doesn't like them, you can still ensure he or she is getting the health benefits they offer by making pancakes or doing some home baking.

Thoughts...
about Meat

These foods are rich in protein, which is essential for building and repairing the body. Of course, if you choose not to eat meat or fish, there are alternatives such as soya and nuts, seeds, beans and pulses which will provide the essential proteins for good health. Indeed, those of us who do eat meat could do worse than to incorporate more of these into our diet, as they are low-fat, cheap and filling.

Red meat is also an important source of iron, which is essential in producing red blood cells.

A protein source should be present in one or two of our meals every day. There are many ways to cook meat ... in a traditional roast, for example, or added to such staples as spaghetti bolognese, lasagne, stews, casseroles or curries. When it comes to red meats, such as beef, the cheaper cuts usually require long, slow cooking in order to become tender, so are perfect for stews and casseroles, which can then be bulked out with lots of vegetables and pulses for extra nutrition.

Chicken is a massively popular source of protein, yet has become controversial in recent times due to concerns about its production. If we're to be honest, the more expensive free range or organic chickens do have the best flavour and texture, and can be an economical choice if used for several meals. A roast chicken can be stripped for salads, sandwiches, stir-fries or curries, and even the bones of a chicken can be boiled up with onions, carrots and herbs for stock.

Fish provides us with essential B vitamins as well as protein ... so your mum was right when she told you it would make you clever!

Fish is very quick and easy to prepare, and often only needs a squeeze of lemon and a sprig of fresh herbs to liven it up. It doesn't have to be fried as fish can easily be baked in foil parcels or steamed, which, as well as being a healthier option, doesn't leave any unpleasant odours lingering around your kitchen for days! Also, don't forget to try shellfish, and the more unusual varieties of fish which are making an appearance in our supermarkets and fishmongers as the cod and haddock stocks get lower.

Pollock and witch are two names to look out for ... and what child could resist the promise of "witch and chips" for tea?

Treats...
and Puddings

What would life be like without a little treat once in a while? Of course, we all know that sugary food should be enjoyed in moderation, but puddings don't have to be a diet disaster.

Fruit and dairy products are incorporated into many popular puddings, such as Eton Mess, fruit fondues, jellies, crumbles, etc. Wholemeal flour and oats can be used in many hot puds and bakes such as flapjacks, and honey or maple syrup can be used as a healthier alternative to white sugar and golden syrup.

Homemade puddings and treats are a lot healthier than shop-bought ones. Just a look at the very long and chemical-laden ingredients list of some buns and cakes tells us that they may not be the healthiest option, whereas a homemade cake containing simply flour, butter, sugar and eggs will provide some health benefits as well as being "naughty but nice"!

Why not sandwich a cake together with some whipped cream and strawberries, or finish off some drop scones with sliced bananas and maple syrup?

Children love helping out with baking cakes and treats, and they can be a great introduction to the kitchen for reluctant young chefs. Who doesn't remember helping to grease cake tins, melt chocolate and hull strawberries as a child? And of course, there's often a bowl or two to lick out afterwards!

By George...
it's Spring!

After the long dark days of winter, the nights get lighter and so do our menus and hopefully our moods!
Spring brings an abundance of reasons to be cheerful ...

The first asparagus of the season; it's gorgeous the traditional way with hollandaise sauce, but what about griddled and dipped into a DIY hollandaise of softly boiled egg with butter and cider vinegar, throwing in a fun element?!

Rhubarb, which can escape its usual crumble topping and be oven roasted, cooked and served with greek yoghurt and honey.

And, of course, new potatoes start to appear. These can be boiled or roasted with olive oil and rosemary. In late spring we enjoy the short season of Jersey Royal new potatoes, grab them while you can as their unique flavour makes them a great accompaniment to a simple cut of fish or meat.

Easter comes along, so you might be baking hot cross buns or making some chocolaty treats for the celebrations. This is the traditional time of year for roast lamb, try studding it with garlic and sprigs of fresh rosemary.

We often get a cheeky glimpse of summer during later spring, so make the most of the occasional hot days and bring the barbecue into service. Homemade burgers and kebabs are simple and delicious and there are some great salads and sauces within the book to complement them!

Those of us who keep chickens (and there are more of us every year!) will be thrilled to find the first eggs appearing in the nesting box. If you don't keep hens yourself, try to befriend someone who does, they will be happy to furnish you with eggs once 'the girls' really get going! You can't beat cooking with fresh eggs (pardon the pun!).

Prawn Cocktail

Ingredients

200g cooked and peeled king prawns
1/4 cucumber
romaine or iceberg lettuce
cress
1 lemon
few cherry tomatoes
2 tablespoons mayonnaise
4 heaped teaspoons tomato sauce
worcestershire sauce
tabasco sauce
paprika
salt and pepper

Serves 2-4

In a bowl, mix together the mayonnaise and tomato sauce. Add the juice of half the lemon, a few shakes of worcestershire sauce and a few drops of tabasco, along with a pinch of salt and pepper. Give it a good stir!

Arrange the salad by cutting and mixing the lettuce with some slices of cucumber, the cress and some halved cherry tomatoes.

Pile the prawns on top of the salad and spoon the 'marie-rose' sauce over the top. Add a sprinkling of paprika and a wedge of lemon and you're ready to go!

Scrummy Tips

A GOOD STARTER OR LIGHT LUNCH WHICH CAN BE MADE MORE IMPRESSIVE BY SIMPLE PRESENTATION.

TRY SERVING THE PRAWN COCKTAIL IN AN EXOTIC SHELL.

Chicken Goujons

Ingredients

400g pack of mini chicken
breast fillets
1 egg, beaten
plain flour
breadcrumbs
olive oil

Serves 2

Pre-heat the oven to 190°C (gas mark 5)

In three separate bowls, display the beaten egg, a little flour and the breadcrumbs. Dip the chicken firstly in the flour, then the egg and lastly the breadcrumbs. Place in an oven dish or tray with a drizzle of olive oil over and under the chicken.

Cook for 30 minutes and you have a tasty dish to serve with salad, pitta bread, mayonnaise or tomato sauce.

Scrummy Tips

IT'S ALL ABOUT THE BREADCRUMBS SO MAKE SURE YOU USE GOOD BREAD! I USE GRANARY OR FRESH BROWN BREAD FROM THE BAKERS AND WHIZZ IN A FOOD PROCESSOR TO FINE CRUMBS. ADD A 25G PACKET OF READY SALTED CRISPS, 25G SESAME SEEDS OR 25G PARMESAN OR ALL TOGETHER AND YOU HAVE A MORE TASTY CRUMB. CHEESY CHICKEN GOUJONS ARE POPULAR IN OUR HOUSE AND WITH SCHOOL FRIENDS!

FOLLOW THE SAME PROCEDURE FOR FISH GOUJONS, USING A PLAIN WHITE FISH; SKINNED, BONED AND CUT INTO STRIPS. FISH DOESN'T TAKE AS LONG TO COOK SO 20 MINUTES SHOULD BE OKAY TO BROWN THE BREADCRUMBS. SERVE WITH TARTARE SAUCE AND FAT CHIPS!

Chicken Wraps

Ingredients

1.6kg chicken
1 lemon
80g butter
salt and pepper
12 flour tortillas
(allowing 2 each)
sliced hard boiled eggs
sliced fresh tomatoes
sliced cucumber
cream cheese
lettuce
fresh basil leaves
grated carrot
grated cheese
mayonnaise

Serves 6

Pre-heat the oven to 190°C (gas mark 5)

Place the chicken in a roasting tray, squeeze over the lemon juice and leave the lemon skins in the tray. Rub over or place knobs of butter over the chicken and season. Put the tray in the oven and roast for one hour, occasionally spooning the juices from the tray over the chicken.

Follow the heating instructions for the tortillas. Arrange on a platter, or in separate bowls, the remaining filling ingredients. You can use all or any of the suggested list plus any other salad varieties.

To prepare the tortillas, spread a line across the centre with the mayonnaise or cream cheese. Build up thin layers of salad and chicken and then finish by folding the tortilla over the bottom of one end of the line. Roll the tortilla into a tube and munch away!

Scrummy Tips

YOU MAY LIKE TO INCLUDE COLD COOKED HAM OR BACON TO ACCOMPANY THE CHICKEN. OR, FOR A TOTALLY DIFFERENT COMBINATION, WHIP UP SOME MARIE-ROSE SAUCE AND FILL WITH PRAWNS AND SMOKED SALMON INSTEAD OF THE MEATS.

Lamb with Feta

Ingredients

300g diced lean lamb
2 shallots, peeled
1 tablespoon olive oil
700ml hot water
2 vegetable stock cubes
250g fresh tomatoes, chopped
1 lemon, chopped
250g new potatoes, chopped
200g feta cheese
salt and pepper

Serves 4

Pre-heat oven to 190°C (gas mark 5)

Chop the shallots and put them in a saucepan or hob safe casserole with the olive oil and fry for a minute. Add the meat and brown.

Chop the tomatoes and lemon ... the whole lemon, including the pith and pips! ... then add to the meat along with the stock cubes and water. Season and bring to the boil.

Turn into a casserole dish if required and place in the oven for a good 40 minutes until the water has reduced and the meat is tender. Add the chopped new potatoes and return to the oven for a further half an hour, at least.

When you're ready to eat, crumble in the feta cheese and leave for 10 minutes before serving. Great with rice and vegetables.

Gremoulade with Cheese

Ingredients

1 small orange
(or 1/2 a large one),
zest and juice
1 lemon, zest and juice
1 clove of garlic
25g flat leaf parsley
200g drained capers
100ml olive oil
150g parmesan block
2 x 150g mozzarella balls

Serves 4

This is so easy and yet so tasty! The combination of the hard and soft cheeses is a surprise in itself.

In a food processor, place the orange and lemon zest and juices, the garlic, parsley, capers and olive oil and blend for a few seconds until you have a roughly chopped sauce. You shouldn't need to season this!

Slice the parmesan and mozzarella and layer it alternately on the plates. Spoon the mixture over, reserving any spare for another dish.

Scrummy Tips

GREMOULADE ALSO MAKES A DELICIOUS FINISH TO A SIMPLE GRILLED WHITE FISH... OR SERVE AS A SAUCE AT A BUFFET OR BBQ.

A LARGE PLATTER OF THE CHEESE WITH GREMOULADE WILL SOON DISAPPEAR AT A PARTY!

Vinaigrette

Ingredients

500ml sunflower oil
200ml olive oil
200ml malt vinegar
100ml balsamic vinegar
100g caster sugar
1 teaspoon english mustard
1 teaspoon french mustard
1 teaspoon grainy mustard
1 teaspoon worcestershire sauce
a pinch of paprika
1 teaspoon dried thyme
salt and pepper

Makes about 1.2 litres

Simply put all the ingredients in a food processor or in a bowl, with a hand blender, and whizz away for a few minutes!

Serve on a fresh tomato or green salad ... or an avocado.

Keep the vinaigrette in a bottle or jar in the fridge, giving it a good shake before use, and it should see you through a few summer parties!

Scrummy Tips

THIS WAS ONCE GIVEN TO ME BY A FRIEND WHO BECAME ADDICTED TO MY VINAIGRETTE!.... SHE WOULD DRIZZLE IT OVER CHEESE ON TOAST BEFORE GRILLING!

FILL SOME PRETTY BOTTLES TO GIVE A PRESENT WITH A DIFFERENCE... I'M SURE IT WILL BE WELL RECEIVED!

Teriyaki Steak Stir Fry

Ingredients

50g teriyaki sauce
250g rump steak
1 teaspoon oil
360g pre-prepared pack of stir fry vegetables and bean sprouts
1 red or orange pepper, thinly sliced

Serves 2

This is a quick and easy supper ...

Trim the steak and thinly slice. Place in a bowl with the sauce and marinate for 2-3 hours if you can.

In a wok or large saucepan, heat the oil and add the meat along with the sauce. Quickly brown the meat and add the vegetables. Fry for a couple of minutes and it's ready to serve!

Scrummy Tips

IF YOU PREFER TO PREPARE YOUR OWN SELECTION OF VEGETABLES THEN THINLY SLICE PEPPERS, MUSHROOMS, BROCCOLI, SPRING ONION, CARROTS, BABY SWEETCORN, MANGE TOUT, BEANSPROUTS, BAMBOO SHOOTS OR WHATEVER TAKES YOUR FANCY!

ADD NOODLES TOO?

Bacon, Leek and Gruyere Tart

Ingredients

225g plain flour
50g lard
50g butter or margarine
2 tablespoons water
100g smoked bacon, cut into strips
1 leek, sliced
100g gruyere cheese, grated
2 medium free-range eggs
150ml milk
salt and pepper

Serves 4

Pre-heat the oven to 190°C (gas mark 5)

Lightly grease a 7" (18cm) flan dish.

Mix the flour and a pinch salt in a baking bowl, adding cubes of the fat, cutting and stirring. Mix the cold water in to form a stiff dough, using your hands to knead and blend the ingredients.

Roll the pastry out onto a lightly floured surface and line the flan dish, ensuring there are no little holes in the pastry.

Fry the bacon lightly and cool. Line the pastry case with half of the cheese then layer on top the bacon and leeks. Beat the eggs and milk together, add a pinch of salt and pepper, and pour into the pastry case. Add the remaining cheese and bake for about 40 minutes until set.

Scrummy Tips

YOU CAN ADD SO MANY DIFFERENT INGREDIENTS TO A TART / QUICHE. TRY SOME COOKED CHICKEN AND MUSHROOMS OR FRESH TOMATOES, BASIL AND MOZZARELLA... OR FLAKED SALMON WITH SPINACH.

Chocolate Fondue

Ingredients

100g good quality plain chocolate (over 70% cocoa solids)
a selection of fresh fruit
dried fruit
biscuits or wafers
marshmallows

cocktail sticks

Serves 6

Slowly heat the chocolate in a bowl over a pan of boiling water.

Prepare the fresh fruit and arrange on a platter, along with any dried fruit, biscuits and marshmallows. Pour the melted chocolate into a small bowl and dive in with the cocktail sticks!

Scrummy Tips

IF PLAIN CHOCOLATE IS TOO RICH FOR YOU THEN USE MILK CHOCOLATE, OR A COMBINATION OF BOTH.

A COLD FRUIT SAUCE DIP WOULD MAKE A REFRESHING CHANGE... COOK SOME STRAWBERRIES OR RASPBERRIES IN A SAUCEPAN WITH A TEASPOON OF SUGAR AND THEN MASH TO A PULP. STRAIN THROUGH A SIEVE AND COOL.

Rice Krispie Squares

Ingredients

150g rice krispies
100g butter
200g marshmallows
1 tablespoon golden syrup

Method

Lightly grease and line a 33 x 23cm tin with greaseproof paper.

Melt the butter in a large saucepan over a low heat, adding the syrup and marshmallows until all melted and bubbling away.

Pour in the rice krispies, take off the heat and stir until evenly covered. Tip the mixture into the lined tin and spread out quickly. Leave in a cool place to set and then cut into squares.

Adults and children alike will soon clear a plate of their old favourites!

Custard Tart

Ingredients

110g plain flour
25g lard
25g margarine or butter
15g caster sugar
salt
15ml cold water
2 eggs
300ml milk
2 tablespoons sugar
grated nutmeg

Method

Pre-heat the oven to 180°C (gas mark 4)

Mix the flour, a pinch of salt and the sugar in a mixing bowl. Rub in the fats and using a knife, cut and stir. Gradually add the water, stirring to form a dough.

Flour a board and turn the dough out, kneading lightly to merge the ingredients. Roll out and line a 7 inch flan tin with the pastry, pressing into the edges and trimming away any excess. Make sure there are no holes!

Line the pastry with greaseproof paper. Weigh it down with baking beans, rice or dried beans and bake in the oven for 15 minutes.

Meanwhile, make the filling. Bring the milk and sugar to the boil in a saucepan. Whisk the eggs in a bowl and pour the hot milk over. Stir and then cool.

Strain the sauce into the pastry case, sprinkle generously with grated nutmeg and bake for a further 20 minutes until set.

Chocolate Meringues

Ingredients

3 large free-range eggs
150g golden caster sugar
2 chocolate flakes, crumbled

Makes 12

Pre-heat your oven to 100°C (gas mark 1)

In two bowls, very carefully split the eggs as you only require the egg whites.

With an electric whisk, whisk the egg whites until they form fairly stiff peaks. Slowly add the sugar, continuing to whisk all the time until the sugar has mixed well.

Fold in the crumbled chocolate flakes and spoon equally onto a baking sheet and place in the oven for one hour. Cool on the baking sheet.

Scrummy Tips

DELICIOUS ON THEIR OWN OR SERVED WITH WHIPPED CREAM AND FRESH FRUIT.

FOR A PAVLOVA, SPOON THE MIXTURE AS A WHOLE ONTO THE BAKING SHEET, WITH A SLIGHTLY HIGHER EDGE AROUND THE OUTSIDE.

FILL WITH WHIPPED CREAM AND FRESH FRUIT.

Chocolate Milkshake

Ingredients

1 litre milk
5 chocolate flakes
2 dessert spoons of chocolate sauce
good quality chocolate ice cream

Serves 4

In a blender, whisk the milk, four crumbled flakes and the sauce. Pour into glasses with a dollop of ice-cream and sprinkle some more chocolate flakes over the top.

Serve with a straw and a spoon to please any child!

By George...
it's Summer!

Glorious summer days bring to mind strawberries, beautiful salads, new potatoes, fresh peas straight from the pod, barbecues, picnics, ice creams ...

Nature provides lots of lovely, cooling foods to be enjoyed in the sunshine. Of course, in Britain, we cannot always rely on the sunshine but that should not deter us from enjoying the best of the summer season. Why not have a picnic indoors if the weather is not kind? Warm salads can be more substantial and filling than the traditional green accompaniment, with the addition of some roasted new potatoes and marinated meats.

Rather than dragging out the rusty old barbecue on only one or two occasions when the sun pokes its head out, try incorporating it into your everyday cooking routine. Marinate some lamb chops in olive oil, rosemary and garlic and get someone to throw them on the barbecue while you boil some new potatoes and dress a green salad. This keeps the kitchen clean, cuts down on washing up and gets the family involved in cooking. Fish can also be done quickly and easily on the barbecue, wrapped in some oiled foil parcels with some fresh herbs and perhaps a squeeze of lemon. Then you can decide whether to eat in or out, depending on the weather.

Summer brings with it a feeling of relaxation that can be reflected in the food we are eating and the way we prepare it; lots of thrown-together feasts, impromptu parties and food that everyone can be involved in making and enjoying together.

Asparagus Spears with DIY Hollandaise

Ingredients

1 bunch of fresh asparagus
2 large free-range eggs
butter
cider vinegar
salt and white pepper
olive oil

Serves 2

Rub a little olive oil into the asparagus and cook on a hot griddle or under a grill for 5 minutes, turning once, until a little charred but still crunchy.

Meanwhile, place the eggs in a saucepan half filled with cold water. Bring the water to the boil and then simmer for 3 minutes.

Remove the eggs from the water and place in egg cups with the asparagus lined up alongside. Carefully tap the shell at the top of the egg and take the top off, showing the yolk. Drop a few drops of the vinegar, a knob of butter and season for the DIY hollandaise sauce ... now, dip in the spears and enjoy!

Scrummy Tips

THIS DISH NOT ONLY MAKES A GREAT HEALTHY SNACK BUT WOULD BE AN IMPRESSIVE DINNER PARTY STARTER!

Red Rice Salad

Ingredients

175g red rice
500ml water
3 lemons
2 limes
1 red onion
25g fresh coriander
few leaves of mint
25g flat leaf parsley
200g feta cheese
2 tomatoes
1 red pepper
100ml olive oil
salt and pepper

Method

In a pan, bring the rice to the boil with the water and then simmer for 20 minutes until the rice is cooked al dente.

Meanwhile, zest the lemon and lime into a large bowl and add the juices from both. Finely chop the coriander, mint and parsley and add to the bowl. Peel and chop finely the onion, red pepper and tomatoes. Crumble in the feta cheese, season and stir in the olive oil.

Drain the rice and run under a cold tap to chill the rice but also to keep it crunchy. Add to the other ingredients, stir well and it's ready to serve!

Scrummy Tips

THIS SALAD IS SO REFRESHING AND IS A GREAT ACCOMPANIMENT TO ANY BBQ, BUFFET OR COLD MEATS.

THE FLAVOURS ARE TOTALLY AMAZING AND WILL KEEP PEOPLE COMING BACK FOR MORE!

Pesto Pasta

Ingredients

250g penne pasta (or any other
dried pasta)
150g pine nuts
100ml olive oil
50g parmesan
50g fresh basil leaves
1 clove garlic
1 tablespoon balsamic vinegar
salt and pepper

Method

Cook the pasta in boiling water for a good 5 minutes until
al dente and then run under a cold tap to cool it. Over-
cooked pasta is useless for this refreshing cold pasta dish!

Dry fry the pine nuts in a pan until they are golden in
colour. Place them in a food processor and roughly chop
them, adding the parmesan, basil and garlic until you have
a rough dry paste. Stir in the olive oil, balsamic vinegar
and seasoning and add to the cooled pasta, tossing it until
the pasta is totally covered.

Scrummy Tips

A SUPERB
ACCOMPANIMENT TO ANY
BUFFET OR BBQ AS A COLD
DISH. THIS PESTO SAUCE
CAN ALSO BE STIRRED INTO
HOT PASTA FOR A WARM
DISH, SPRINKLED WITH
PARMESAN SHAVINGS.

Baked Pesto Salmon

Ingredients

50g basil leaves
150g pine nuts, toasted
as below
1 lemon
50g grated parmesan
100ml olive oil
balsamic glaze
salt and pepper
50g breadcrumbs (see pg 28)
4 salmon fillets

Serves 4

Pre-heat the oven to 190°C (gas mark 5)

In a food processor, quickly blend the basil leaves, toasted pine nuts, the zest of the lemon, parmesan, a generous slug of olive oil and a drizzle of balsamic glaze. You should have a nice thick chunky paste. If it looks too dry then add some more oil.

Place the salmon in an oven dish, spread the pesto over the top of each fillet and sprinkle a generous covering of breadcrumbs over the tops. Season with a pinch of salt and pepper and bake in the oven for 15 minutes until the salmon is cooked and the breadcrumbs are golden.

Serve with new potatoes, seasonal vegetables and a wedge of lemon.

Scrummy Tips

TO TOAST THE PINE NUTS, SIMPLY DRY FRY OVER A LOW HEAT TURNING TO LIGHTLY BROWN ALL SIDES. THIS MAKES SUCH A DIFFERENCE TO THE FLAVOUR OF THE PESTO!

Coronation Chicken

Ingredients

4 chicken breasts
1 tablespoon olive oil
50ml water
salt and pepper
300g mayonnaise
1 teaspoon grainy mustard
1 teaspoon worcestershire sauce
1 teaspoon dried thyme
1 teaspoon paprika
50g flaked almonds
100g sultanas
400g tin cubed pineapple, drained
400g tin sliced mango, peaches or apricots, drained
20g fresh chives, chopped
6 spring onions, chopped
1 lemon
2 teaspoons medium curry powder

Serves 4

Pre-heat the oven to 190°C (gas mark 5)

Put the chicken, oil, water and seasoning in an oven dish and cook in the oven for half an hour. Lift the chicken out onto a board and cool thoroughly.

Mix all the other ingredients in a mixing bowl along with the zest and juice of the lemon. Slice and add the chicken once cool and mix well.

Scrummy Tips

I LOVE THIS COLD DISH WITH SALAD BUT IT EASILY ADAPTS TO A WARM DISH BY SIMPLY ADDING A BREADCRUMB TOPPING TO THE MIXTURE, IN AN OVEN DISH, AND BAKING FOR 30 MINUTES.

Tomato & Mozzarella Canapés

Ingredients

buffalo mozzarella or
mozzarella pearls
cherry tomatoes, halved
fresh basil leaves
whole pitted black olives
balsamic glaze

cocktail sticks

Method

Simply thread chunks of mozzarella, halved tomatoes, folded basil leaves and black olives onto the cocktail sticks. Arrange on a platter and drizzle a little balsamic glaze over.

A colourful Scooby snack for all ages!

Scrummy Tips

COCKTAIL STICKS ARE GREAT FUN FOR CHILDREN BEING CREATIVE. TRY THE TRADITIONAL CUBES OF CHEESE AND PINEAPPLE OR PRAWNS WITH FOLDED MANGE TOUT AND MANGO.

OR EVEN TRY A MINI FRUIT KEBAB!

Eton Mess

Ingredients

8 meringues, crumbled
(shop-bought is ok)
300ml double cream
70g caster sugar
450g fresh strawberries, hulled
and sliced
1 teaspoon rose water
icing sugar

Serves 4

In a saucepan, gently heat and simmer 50g of the strawberries with 20g of caster sugar. Mash to a jam and cool.

Whisk up the cream with remaining caster sugar, add the crumbled meringues and mix in the rest of the sliced strawberries.

Stir the rose water into the jam when it is cold and carefully fold into the cream and meringues.

Serve in individual bowls, or in a large serving bowl and sprinkle with some icing sugar.

Scrummy Tips

THIS PUDDING CAN BE
ADAPTED FOR
RASPBERRIES,
BLACKBERRIES
OR OTHER SOFT SUMMER
FRUITS... OR A
COMBINATION OF ALL!

Strawberry
Jam
06/08

Strawberry Jam

Ingredients

2kg strawberries, hulled
1kg jam sugar
1 lemon
1 knob of butter

Makes 4 450g Jars

Place the strawberries in a large saucepan with the zest and juice of the lemon. Add the sugar and bring to the boil, stirring well. Boil for 25 minutes, stir in the butter and then cool. Pour into 4 hot sterilised jam jars.

Scrummy Tips

A GREAT PRESENT FOR A FRIEND OR RELATIVE... WHAT'S NICER THAN RECEIVING SOMETHING HOMEMADE?

MAYBE BAKE A FEW SCONES TO GO WITH IT?

Raspberry Cream Sponge Cake

Ingredients

150g self-raising flour
150g butter or margarine
150g golden caster sugar
1 teaspoon baking powder
1 teaspoon vanilla extract
3 large free-range eggs

1 tablespoon raspberry jam
400g fresh raspberries
250ml double cream
1 tablespoon caster sugar
icing sugar

Scrummy Tips

YOU CAN USE MOST SOFT
FRUITS FOR THIS CAKE...
TRY STIRRING SOME COOLED
MELTED CHOCOLATE INTO
THE CREAM FOR A
CHOCOLATE CREAM FILLING
OR REPLACE 25G OF THE
FLOUR FOR 25G COCOA
POWDER FOR A CHOCOLATE
CAKE!
THE SAME CAKE MIXTURE
WILL FILL AROUND 24 BUN
CASES... BAKE FOR AROUND
10 MINUTES UNTIL GOLDEN,
AS BEFORE, THEN ONCE
COOLED YOU CAN ICE AND
DECORATE THEM WITH
SPRINKLES, CHERRIES ETC.

Serves 6

Pre-heat the oven to 180°C (gas mark 4)

Line 2 x 8" (20cm) loose-based sandwich tins with greaseproof paper and lightly grease.

Into a mixing bowl, sieve the flour and baking powder, add the sugar, butter or margarine and then the vanilla extract and the eggs. With an electric hand whisk, blend until you have a smooth creamy texture.

Split the mixture between the two tins and bake in the oven for 25 minutes until you have a lightly golden coloured cake. Cool on a baking rack.

When you're ready to fill the cake, carefully warm the jam in a saucepan over a low heat and spread it over the base of your cake.

Layer the raspberries over the top and then whip up the cream and caster sugar with an electric whisk. Spread over the raspberries, place the other cake on top and give the cake a good sprinkling of icing sugar, with a sieve.

Sally's Jelly Slice

Ingredients

250g packet of Nice biscuits
(or other plain type)
100g unsalted butter, melted
1 sachet powdered gelatine
175ml water
400g tin condensed milk
juice of 2 lemons
1 packet strawberry jelly
300ml boiling water
150ml cold water

Serves 10

Carefully melt the butter in a saucepan. Crush the biscuits in a food processor and mix with the melted butter. Press into a 'brownie' tin and chill to set. For wedges like a cheesecake, a 25cm flan dish will do the same trick.

Once the biscuit base is set you can make the middle layer. Dissolve the gelatine in the water then combine with the condensed milk and lemon juice. It will look curdled but stir well and don't worry, it will set perfectly. Pour over the biscuit base and chill until set.

For the third layer, dissolve the strawberry jelly in the boiling water, add the cold water and stand until cool. Pour over the lemon mixture and chill until set.

Cut into individual portions to serve.

Scrummy Tips

KATIE IS WONDERING ABOUT LIME JUICE IN THE MIDDLE LAYER WITH LIME JELLY ON TOP ... OR WITH AN ORANGE FLAVOUR MAYBE?

Kindly donated by

Richard Cawley

Crunchie Ice Cream for Cheats

Ingredients

1 litre tub of good quality
vanilla ice cream
300g toffee sauce or crème du
luce
160g crunchie bars (5), crushed
150g brandy snaps, crushed
150ml double cream

Method

Should I be letting you in on this one? I'm not sure!!

Soften the ice cream slightly in a large bowl, add the toffee
sauce, the double cream and the crushed up crunchie bars
and brandy snaps.

Give it a good stir, pour it back into the tub and freeze for
whenever takes your fancy! They'll be coming back for
more …. and more

Scrummy Tips

THIS MAKES A GREAT
ALTERNATIVE TO PLAIN
VANILLA ICE-CREAM,
SERVED ON TOP OF AN
APPLE CRUMBLE... OR
GREAT INSIDE A BRANDY
SNAP BASKET WITH FRESH
SUMMER FRUIT

Summer Fruits & White Choc Sauce

Ingredients

400g frozen summer berries
300ml double cream
70g packet of white chocolate buttons
1 vanilla pod

Serves 4

When you're ready to serve your pudding, evenly line your dishes or plates with the frozen fruit.

In a saucepan, gently heat the cream and chocolate buttons. Scrape in some seeds from the vanilla pod and stir until the chocolate has melted and you have a hot thick sauce. Pour into a warmed jug and serve to your guests at the table, pouring the sauce over the fruit. The heat will defrost the fruit and give a hot and cold twist to an easy attractive pudding.

Scrummy Tips

IF THE FRUIT IS PARTICULARLY LARGE YOU MAY NEED TO LET IT STAND A FEW MINUTES TO DE-FROST SLIGHTLY BEFORE SERVING.

BBQ Sauce

Ingredients

2 oranges
2 teaspoons worcestershire sauce
1 teaspoon english mustard
tabasco sauce
$1/2$ teaspoon ground paprika
1 clove garlic
4 tablespoons runny honey
3 tablespoons tomato sauce
salt and pepper

Method

In a food processor, blend together the orange zest, the juice from the oranges, a few shakes of tabasco sauce and all the other ingredients. Simple as that!!

This BBQ sauce is so versatile and can be used as a marinade for different meats but here are two ideas ...

Pork and Apricot Kebabs

400g diced pork,
marinated in the sauce for a couple of hours
150g dried apricots
1 red or orange pepper, cubed
1 red onion, cut into chunks

Wet a few wooden kebab sticks and thread the pork, apricots, pepper and onion alternatively, repeating the process two or three times. Cook on the BBQ for 5-10 minutes, turning occasionally and brushing over some of the remaining sauce.

Spare Ribs (are there ever any spare?!)

500g rack of pork ribs

Carefully cut the rack of ribs into individuals, if required, and marinate them in the BBQ sauce, again for a couple of hours at least. As before, cook on the BBQ and brush with some extra sauce if required.

Scrummy Tips

IF IT'S RAINING OUTSIDE, THERE'S NO HARM IN COOKING THESE IN THE OVEN IN AN OVEN DISH!

Burgers & Corn on the Cob

Ingredients

800g minced beef
plain flour

4 corn on the cobs
25g butter

Serves 8

Roll the mince into golf balls, slightly squash to flatten and roll into a little flour. Your burgers are ready to cook on the BBQ or on a griddle.

Pre-heat the oven to 190°C (gas mark 5)

Cut the corn in half and place in an oven dish. Roast with the butter for 10 minutes to help the process along.

Remove from the oven and finish off on the BBQ for 5 minutes, brushing any remaining butter over whilst turning.

Baked Peaches & Bananas

Ingredients

4 fresh peaches
25g butter
8 amaretto biscuits, crushed
4 tablespoons maple syrup

4 bananas
70g milk chocolate buttons

Serves 4

Both these puddings can be cooked, wrapped in foil, on the BBQ or in an oven dish with a temperature of 190°C (gas mark 5).

Cut the peaches in half, removing the stone, and place in an oven dish, cut side up. Fill the holes with the syrup and sprinkle the biscuits over each half. Add a knob of butter to each and any remaining syrup or butter to the dish. Cover with foil and bake for one hour.

Make a long slit through the skin and flesh of each banana, slotting in the chocolate buttons as you go. Wrap them in foil and bake for half an hour.

By George...
it's Autumn!

The nights are drawing in and we say goodbye to the long summer days. What's to smile about? Well, there's plenty! Old familiar faces such as carrots, broccoli, cauliflower and parsnips are in season, ready to warm us up and sustain us for the long, cold months ahead. In general, those foods that take longer to grow are the most warming... isn't nature clever!

Of course, a long list of vegetables can be pretty uninspiring, so try to be a bit adventurous with them. Cauliflower is great in a curry, broccoli stir-fries or roasts beautifully with a bit of chilli and garlic, and who can resist honeyed carrots or roast parsnips nestling next to a lemony roast chicken?

There are plenty of events to cheer us up as we wave goodbye to summer... Hallowe'en, when pumpkins come into their own, of course! Try making a soup or a pumpkin pie for a Hallowe'en party. You can also get creative in the kitchen making gruesome party treats to freak out your friends and family. Green jelly often comes in handy at this time of year!

Bonfire Night means wrapping up and cradling either a mug of hot soup, a baked potato, bangers (of both varieties!), or a bowl of chilli... and, of course, parkin, toffee apples and bonfire toffee.

Autumn also brings with it the apple harvest, and that means beautiful crumbles, pies and tarts. Try collecting blackberries to put into them... there's something very satisfying about cooking and eating something you have picked yourself – especially free of charge!

Pasta Bake

Ingredients

Serves 4

3 tomatoes, sliced
340g tin of sweetcorn, drained
4/6 rashers of bacon
125g mozzarella cheese
250g dried penne pasta
40g butter
2 tablespoons plain flour
500ml milk
150g cheddar cheese, grated
50g parmesan cheese, grated
salt and pepper

Pre-heat the oven to 190°C (gas mark 5)

Grill or fry the bacon until cooked and tear into pieces. Place in an oven dish along with the sliced tomatoes and sweetcorn. Also, tear in pieces of mozzarella.

Bring a large saucepan of water to the boil and add the dried pasta. Let it simmer for 10 minutes, drain and mix into the other ingredients in the oven dish.

Meanwhile, melt the butter in a saucepan over a low heat, then add the flour, stirring well with a wooden spoon and adding the milk slowly whilst still stirring. You will soon see a paste forming, hopefully with no lumps! Whisk any out with a hand whisk.

Turn up the heat and add the grated cheddar cheese, salt and pepper. Once you have a thick even sauce pour it over the pasta, sprinkle the top with the grated parmesan and bake in the oven for 30 minutes.

Scrummy Tips

SWAP THE BACON AND SWEETCORN FOR HAM AND PEAS... AND THE TOMATOES FOR MUSHROOMS?

THIS IS A GREAT RECIPE FOR PLAYING AROUND WITH!

Fish Pie

Ingredients

300g fresh skinless and
boneless salmon
300g fresh skinless and
boneless cod
300g fresh skinless and
boneless smoked haddock
325g tin sweetcorn, drained
100g fresh or frozen peas
200g peeled king prawns
40g butter
2 tablespoons plain flour
500ml milk
150g cheddar cheese
salt and pepper
1kg potatoes (I use maris piper)
50g butter for the potatoes
200ml milk
olive oil

Serves 6

Pre-heat the oven to 190°C (gas mark 5)

Peel and cut the potatoes, bringing them to the boil in a large pan of salted water. Cook for about 35 minutes until soft.

Cut the fish into chunks and place in a large oven dish along with the drained sweetcorn, peas and prawns.

In a saucepan, melt the butter over a low heat, then add the flour, stirring well with a wooden spoon and adding the milk slowly whilst stirring. You will soon see a paste forming, hopefully with no lumps! Whisk any out with a hand whisk.

Turn the heat up and add the grated cheese, salt and pepper. Once you have a thick even sauce pour it over the fish.

Once the potatoes are soft, drain them and add the butter and milk. Mash to a smooth creamy texture then spread over the fish sauce. For a rosti topping, peal and grate another potato over the topping. Add a drizzle of oil and bake in the oven for 40 minutes until the top is crispy and golden.

Serve with fresh green vegetables or simply on its own.

Scrummy Tips

IF YOU LIKE HARD BOILED EGGS IN YOUR FISH PIE THEN LAYER SLICES ON TOP OF THE FISH AND CHEESE SAUCE MIXTURE, BEFORE ADDING THE POTATOES.

Chicken Surprise

Ingredients

4 chicken breasts
100g/4 slices ham
150g mozzarella cheese
breadcrumbs (see page 28)
1 egg, beaten
plain flour
olive oil

cocktail sticks

Serves 4

Pre-heat the oven to 190°C (Gas mark 5).

Flatten the chicken breasts by placing on a wooden board and bashing with a meat hammer or rolling pin.

Place a slice of ham in the centre of the chicken along with a $1/4$ of the mozzarella. Carefully wrap the chicken around the filling, securing the parcel with cocktail sticks if you need a helping hand.

In three separate bowls, display the beaten egg, a little flour and the breadcrumbs. Roll the chicken firstly in the flour, then the egg and lastly the breadcrumbs. Place in an oven dish with a drizzle of olive oil over and under the chicken. Cook for 40 minutes and look forward to the surprise of cutting into the chicken with the oozing cheese!

Scrummy Tips

TRY REPLACING THE HAM AND CHEESE FOR A SIMPLE STUFFING MIXTURE. THERE ARE ALL SORTS OF VARIETIES AVAILABLE IF YOU DON'T FANCY MAKING YOUR OWN! FOLLOW THE INSTRUCTIONS ON THE PACKET AND ONCE MIXED WITH WATER, ADD TO THE CENTRE OF YOUR CHICKEN.

Cottage Pie

Ingredients

800g lean mince steak
1kg potatoes (I use maris piper)
250g carrots
1 onion
1 courgette
500ml boiling water
1 beef stock cube
1 teaspoon grainy mustard
1 teaspoon worcestershire sauce
1 tablespoon brown sauce
50g butter
200ml cream
salt and pepper

Serves 6

Peel the potatoes and bring them to the boil in salted water, cooking for about 35 minutes until soft.

Meanwhile brown the mince in a large pan. Peel the carrots and onion and, along with the courgette, finely chop in a food processor. Add to the meat and season.

Add the water, stock cube, mustard, worcestershire sauce and brown sauce to the meat. Cover and simmer for a good 30 minutes until tender. Lift the meat out with a slotted spoon and place in a large oven dish, with some of the gravy. Any remaining liquid can be retained and heated for serving.

Once the potatoes are soft, drain them and add the butter and cream. Mash to a smooth creamy texture then loosely but evenly spread over the meat. Add a drizzle of olive oil and bake in the oven for 50 minutes until the topping is brown and crispy.

Simply serve with peas and broccoli.

Scrummy Tips

THE CREAM IN THE MASHED POTATO CAN BE EXCHANGED FOR MILK IF IT IS A LITTLE TOO RICH!

Baked Butternut Squash

Ingredients

2 butternut squashes
50g breadcrumbs
50g sultanas
1 lemon
1 apple
50g couscous
1 onion
50g pinenuts
400g tin chick peas, drained
150ml water
1 teaspoon paprika
100g feta cheese
salt and pepper
1 tablespoon olive oil

Serves 4

Pre-heat the oven to 190°C (gas mark 5)

Slice the squash lengthways into half and scoop out the seeds. If you need a bigger hole then take out some of the flesh also. Place in an oven dish.

With the help of a food processor, whiz down the bread to fine crumbs and put in a mixing bowl. Also finely chop individually, the apple, chick peas and onion and add each to the bowl. Zest the lemon and mix in, along with the juice. Crumble in the feta cheese and stir in the remaining ingredients, give it a good mix and fill the squash with a good helping.

Drizzle over the oil and cover with tin foil. Bake in the oven for one hour, remove the foil and cook for a further 10 minutes until slightly browned.

Scrummy Tips

THERE ARE SO MANY PRETTY AND UGLY VARIETIES OF SQUASH AND ALL CAN BE USED FOR THIS DISH. OR, MAYBE EVEN A MARROW OR PUMPKIN?

Mushroom & Bacon Risotto

Ingredients

olive oil
100g smoked bacon, cut into strips
250g mushrooms, peeled and sliced
200g risotto rice
100g fresh peas
2 vegetable stock cubes
worcestershire sauce
50g grated parmesan
3 spring onions, chopped
salt and pepper

Serves 4-6

Stir the stock cubes into a jug of 800ml hot water until dissolved.

In a large saucepan or wok, on a medium heat, drizzle a little olive oil. Add the strips of smoked bacon and fry for a minute. Add the mushrooms, peas and the rice and stir until the rice is coated in the oils. Shake in a few drops of worcestershire sauce and add a pinch of salt and pepper.

Gradually add the stock and keep stirring for 20 minutes until you have a rich creamy consistency and the rice has absorbed the stock. The rice should still be soft and runny.

Take off the heat, add the chopped spring onions and grated parmesan and give it a good stir. Wait a couple of minutes before serving.

Scrummy Tips

RISOTTO IS VERY VERSATILE. TRY REPLACING THE BACON FOR CHICKEN AND THE MUSHROOMS FOR LEEKS OR ASPARAGUS.

Honeyed Sausages in a Box

Ingredients

12 chipolata sausages
4 tablespoons runny honey
2 teaspoons sesame seeds
1 teaspoon olive oil
1 granary loaf, unsliced

Method

Pre-heat the oven to 190°C (gas mark 5)

Cut the sausages into two and roast in an oven dish along with the other ingredients for 25 minutes, until brown.

Cut off the lid and scoop out the centre of the loaf of bread, keeping the inside for future breadcrumbs. Line with greaseproof paper.

The sausages can go straight inside the bread box, ready to hand out for any occasion.

Scrummy Tips

MIX TOGETHER SOME MAYONNAISE AND GRAINY MUSTARD TO GIVE A GORGEOUS SIMPLE DIP TO COMPLIMENT THE SAUSAGES.

Autumn Soup

Ingredients

800g sweet potatoes
800g parsnips
400g onion
800g carrots
1 large orange
olive oil
2 vegetable stock cubes
2 litres hot water
salt and pepper
fresh coriander

Method

Peel and chop into chunks the sweet potatoes, parsnips, onion and carrots. Place in a large saucepan with a little olive oil and lightly coat the vegetables over a low heat.

Zest the orange and add to the pan, with the juice.

Mix the stock cubes with the hot water and pour into the pan with a good pinch of salt and pepper. Turn up the heat and bring to the boil. Turn the heat down slightly and simmer for approx 35 minutes until the vegetables are tender.

With a hand blender, or in a food processor, whiz down the vegetables to a smooth soup. Taste and add any more seasoning if required.

Add some chopped coriander just before serving.

Scrummy Tips

SOUPS ARE SO EASY AND YOU CAN PLAY AROUND WITH ALL SORTS OF WONDERFUL VEGETABLES. TRY LEEKS AND POTATOES TOGETHER OR A VARIETY OF MUSHROOMS.

FOR A TASTY SIMPLE TOMATO SOUP, ROAST THE TOMATOES IN THE OVEN WITH SOME ONION AND FRESH THYME.
ADD TO THE BOILING STOCK, SEASON AND WHIZ DOWN.

Apple Crumble

Ingredients

75g porridge oats
75g plain flour
75g golden caster sugar
75g butter, cut into pieces
100g sultanas
900g cooking apples
1 lemon

Serves 4

Pre-heat the oven to 190°C (gas mark 5).

Place the porridge oats, flour, sugar and butter into a bowl and rub together to form even crumbs.

Peel, core and slice the apples into an oven dish. Add the zest and the juice of the lemon along with the sultanas and mix well.

Layer the crumble mixture evenly over the top and cook for 35 minutes until golden brown and the fruit is soft.

Serve with custard, cream or ice cream... or all three if you like!

Scrummy Tips

FOR A LITTLE VARIATION, ADD A FEW SLICES OF STEM GINGER AND A LITTLE OF THE SYRUP TO THE FRUIT... OR A FEW BLACKBERRIES,... OR SOME SLICED PLUMS.

Chocolate Banana Loaf

Ingredients

75g butter or margarine
110g golden caster sugar
1 large free-range egg, beaten
225g plain flour
2 teaspoons baking powder
4 bananas, peeled
1 orange, zest only
1 lemon, zest only
50g chopped walnuts
2 chocolate flakes, crumbled

Method

Pre-heat the oven to 180°C (gas mark 4)

Grease a loaf tin (19 x 9cm) and line with greaseproof paper. Grease the paper also.

Mash the bananas in a bowl with a fork.

Soften the butter and place in another mixing bowl with the sugar, beaten egg, flour and baking powder. With an electric whisk, blend the ingredients. Add the orange and lemon zest, walnuts, bananas and chocolate and whisk again.

Pour the mixture into the tin and bake for 55 minutes until golden and springy to touch. Leave to cool then slice and spread with butter.

Scrummy Tips

TRY REPLACING THE BANANAS WITH ANOTHER FRUIT, WHOLE BLUEBERRIES OR RASPBERRIES OR FINELY CHOPPED APPLE OR PEACH?

Almond Biscotti

Ingredients

120g blanched almonds
250g plain flour
125g caster sugar
1 level teaspoon baking powder
2 large free-range eggs plus
1 yolk
$1/2$ teaspoon almond essence

Method

Pre-heat the oven to 180°C (gas mark 4)

Toast the almonds on a baking tray for 10 minutes until browned. Cool and reserve 30g of the whole nuts. Chop the remaining nuts in a food processor until you have a fine powder.

Mix the ground nuts in a mixing bowl with the flour, sugar and baking powder. Add the almond essence, beat in the eggs and yolk and mix in the remaining whole nuts. With your hands, knead the mixture well until you have a thick dough.

Divide the mixture in two and roll each into a long sausage, about 30cm in length. Flatten the tops to make more of a log effect and place them apart on a baking sheet. Bake for 25 minutes until golden and hard on the outside.

Remove from the oven and cool for a few minutes. Transfer the logs to a board and carefully cut them on a diagonal angle into 1cm thick slices. Re-arrange the slices, cut side up, on the baking sheet and bake for a further 10 minutes.

Cool and then store in an airtight container or jar... ready to dip into a hot chocolate or coffee.

Scrummy Tips

IF YOU CAN'T GET ALMOND ESSENCE THEN USE VANILLA ESSENCE. TRY USING HAZELNUTS INSTEAD OF ALMONDS OR EVEN STIR IN A FEW CHUNKS OF CHOCOLATE.

Gingerbread Families

Ingredients

300g self-raising flour
100g golden caster sugar
50g butter or margarine
3 tablespoons golden syrup
3 teaspoons ground ginger
4 tablespoons milk
pinch of salt

Method

Pre-heat the oven to 160°C (gas mark 3)

Grease a baking tray.

Place the flour, salt and ginger in a bowl. In a saucepan, melt the sugar, fat and golden syrup then add the syrup to the dry ingredients. Mix well, adding the milk and then kneading the gingerbread carefully with your hands.

Roll the gingerbread out with a rolling pin and use cutters to form your families. Place on the baking tray, adding any currants or cherries for eyes, buttons and mouths.

Bake for 10-15 minutes and then cool on a baking rack. Decorate with coloured icing... if you can catch them!

Scrummy Tips

THE SAME MIXTURE CAN BE CUT INTO STARS AND CHRISTMAS SHAPES (MAKING A SMALL HOLE TO THREAD A RIBBON THROUGH LATER), WITH A LITTLE MILK BRUSHED OVER BEFORE BAKING. THESE MAKE INTERESTING DECORATIONS.

By George...
it's Winter!

You cannot think of winter in the kitchen without thinking about warming stews, casseroles and roasts. It is the time of year when root vegetables, such as parsnips, carrots and swedes are in season.

These lend themselves not only to stews, where they add flavour and richness to the gravy; but also to trays of delicious roasted vegetables; an easy accompaniment to a roast, which look and taste far more impressive than the preparation time would have you believe.

Some farm shops are now starting to stock an impressive array of unusual winter squashes. Although rather challenging on the appearance front, try not to be put off, as these can also be roasted or made into rich, healthy soups.

Of course, those cold winter days cry out for hot puddings (any excuse!). Dried fruits can be made into delicious homemade mincemeat for mince pies or for stuffing apples stored from the autumn harvest. Crumbles, pies and sponge puddings all come into their own when long winter evenings stretch ahead and we all need a bit of comfort to warm our cockles!

Winter is also a time when cooks start to think about entertaining guests at Christmas and New Year. Old favourites, such as cocktail sausages (can anyone contemplate a party without these?) can be given a bit of a boost with honey and sesame seeds and presented in a homemade bread box. More adventurous hosts may wish to enter the world of canapés. These can be quick and easy, and little people in the kitchen tend to like doing the fiddly bits, especially those involving cocktail sticks... so, why not let them? Let's face it, during the festive season, we need all the help we can get...

Steak & Tomato Pasta

Ingredients

2 x 400g tins of chopped
tomatoes
1 x 500g jar/packet of tomato
passata
500g braising or rump steak,
cubed
4 tomatoes
1 red pepper
1 onion
1 red onion
1 clove garlic
1 tablespoon tomato purée
salt and pepper
dried oregano

Serves 6

Pre-heat oven to 150°C (gas mark 2)

In a hob friendly casserole dish (or a saucepan) brown the
meat for a few minutes.

In a food processor finely chop the fresh tomatoes, onions,
garlic and red pepper. Add the vegetables to the casserole,
along with the chopped tomatoes, passata, tomato puree,
seasoning and a generous sprinkling of the dried oregano.

Bring to the boil and place in the oven for a good 4/5
hours, stirring occasionally. I know it's a long time but if
you have a slow cooker then it's a quick recipe to throw
together at the start of the day and come home to later!

Serve with pasta and grated parmesan and a chunk of
bread.

Scrummy Tips

I WOULD NORMALLY COOK
THIS SAUCE WITH 1/3RD OF
A BOTTLE OF RED WINE! IT
GIVES IT A MUCH RICHER
SAUCE. SWAP ONE TIN OF
TOMATOES FOR THE WINE!!

Lasagne

Ingredients

300g dried lasagne (no pre-cook)
450g tomatoes
1 red onion, peeled
1-2 cloves garlic, peeled
1 red pepper
fresh or dried thyme
olive oil
salt and pepper
500g lean minced beef
1 tablespoon tomato purée
40g butter
2 tablespoons plain flour
500ml milk
75g grated parmesan
150g grated mozzarella

Scrummy Tips

SIMPLY SERVE WITH A SALAD AND TASTY BREADS. THE RAGU MIXTURE IS THE BOLOGNESE IN SPAGHETTI BOLOGNESE SO MAKE EXTRA AND FREEZE IT FOR A QUICK FUTURE SUPPER. ALSO, THE ROASTED VEG, STRAIGHT FROM THE OVEN AND WHIZZED DOWN IN THE FOOD PROCESSOR, IS DELICIOUS SIMPLY SERVED ON TOP OF FRESHLY COOKED PASTA WITH GRATED PARMESAN.

Serves 4-6

Pre-heat the oven to 190°C (gas mark 5)

Roughly chop the tomatoes, red onion, garlic and red pepper and place on an oven tray along with some olive oil, salt, pepper and a few sprigs of thyme. Cook for 35 minutes until the flavours have mingled. Place in a food processor and you have a delightful sauce.

Brown the mince for 5 minutes in a large saucepan whilst the vegetables are in the oven then add the sauce, along with the tomato purée. This is called a 'ragu'.

You can also make the bechamel sauce when all that is going on! Simply, melt the butter in a saucepan over a low heat, then add the flour, stirring well with a wooden spoon and adding the milk slowly whilst still stirring. You will soon see a paste forming, hopefully with no lumps! Whisk any out with a hand whisk.

With your oven dish at the ready, spread about $1/4$ of the ragu in the bottom, place a layer of the dried lasagne sheets on top and then $1/5$ of the sauce. Sprinkle some of the mozzarella and parmesan and repeat the process 3 more times so you have 4 layers of each process. The last layer should allow $2/5$ of the sauce to cover the whole of the top. Finish with a generous sprinkle of mozzarella and parmesan and bake in the oven for 40 minutes until bubbling away.

Mad Hatter's Meatballs

Ingredients

20g butter or 40ml olive oil
1 green pepper, chopped
1 small onion, peeled and
chopped
400g carton of tomato soup
1 teaspoon sugar
1 tablespoon tomato purée
300ml water
1 egg, beaten
900g minced beef, pork, lamb
or chicken
2 slices of bread made into
breadcrumbs
60ml condensed milk
salt and pepper

Serves 6

Melt the butter in a frying pan and add the chopped pepper and onion, stirring until tender.

Add to the mixture, the tomato soup, sugar, tomato purée and water. Heat until the sauce is gently boiling then turn down the temperature and slowly simmer the sauce, stirring occasionally.

While the sauce is cooking, make the meatballs. Add the beaten egg to the minced meat, mix in the breadcrumbs and condensed milk and season. Roll the meat into balls the size of golf balls and carefully spoon them into the simmering sauce. Cook slowly for one hour until cooked.

Serve with rice, pasta or mashed potatoes.

Kindly donated by

Colin Alderson

Thai Lamb

Ingredients

300g diced lean lamb
1 tablespoon olive oil
2 shallots, peeled
1 lemon grass
1 square inch fresh ginger, peeled
1 garlic clove
2 limes
1 large carrot, peeled
4 cardamon pods
1 teaspoon cumin seeds
2 heaped teaspoons red thai curry paste
2 heaped teaspoons tamarind paste
1 teaspoon fish sauce
1 chicken stock cube
400ml hot water
1 cinnamon stick
400ml tin coconut milk
salt and pepper
1 teaspoon sugar
250g potatoes, peeled
25g fresh coriander, chopped
50g cashew nuts or peanuts

Serves 4

Pre-heat the oven to 190°C (gas mark 5)

Prepare your ingredients first... in a pan, dry fry the cardamon pods and cumin seeds for a few minutes and then crush with a spoon (or pestle and mortar).

In a food processor, chop finely the peeled shallots, lemon grass, peeled ginger, garlic and carrot.

Now, heat the oil in a saucepan (or hob safe casserole) and brown the lamb. Add the cardamon and cumin, the red thai paste and tamarind paste. Stir well, adding the onion and ginger mixture, the fish sauce, stock cube, water and coconut milk. Stir in the zest and juice of one of the limes. Bring to the boil, season and add the sugar. Also add the cinnamon stick.

Place the lamb in a casserole, if required, and cook in the oven for 40 minutes.

Add the chopped potatoes and return to the oven for an hour until the potatoes are soft and meat is tender. Remove the cinnamon stick.

When ready to serve, stir in the chopped coriander, cashew nuts and add the juice of the other lime.

Side dish

Simply serve with thai jasmine rice and pickled cucumber...

1 cucumber
1 shallot
200ml water
3 tablespoons white wine vinegar
2 tablespoons sugar
1 small red chilli, de-seeded

Slice the cucumber and layer in a dish. Put all the other ingredients in a food processor, then pour over the cucumber. Cover and chill in a fridge for at least 3 hours.

Smoked Salmon Parcels

Ingredients

200g smoked salmon
150g fresh prawns
100g smoked mackerel fillets, skinned
100g cream cheese
1 lemon
drizzle of olive oil
fresh dill
pepper (no salt needed!)

Serves 4

You'll need 4 ramekins for your moulds. Line them with cling film, leaving plenty to fold over later.

For presentation, inside the ramekin you can put a drizzle of olive oil, a small wedge of lemon and a small sprig of dill. When the parcel is turned out this gives a lovely finish.

Line the ramekin with the salmon, leaving no gaps and pressing down into the edges. Keep enough hanging over to close the parcel.

In a food processor, blend together the remaining ingredients, along with the remaining lemon zest and juice of the lemon. You'll only need a few sprigs of the dill as it has a strong taste. If you have extra salmon, from buying a larger quantity, then you can put some in the mousse.

Dollop a large teaspoon of mixture inside each ramekin and fold over the salmon to close the parcel. Fold the cling film, pressing down, and stack the ramekins in the fridge for a few hours until ready. This is a great dish to make the day before and will make a beautiful starter or light lunch, served with a simple salad of watercress and some wheaten bread.

Scrummy Tips

ANY REMAINING MOUSSE CAN BE USED ON TOAST AS A SNACK OR COULD BECOME ANOTHER STARTER IN THE FORM OF BRUSCHETTA.

SLICE FRENCH BREAD THINLY, ON AN ANGLE, BRUSH OVER A LITTLE OIL AND BAKE IN THE OVEN UNTIL CRISPY.

Artichoke Dip

Ingredients

1 onion
1 clove of garlic
100g parmesan
2 x 400g tins of artichokes, drained
1 x 400g tin of mixed beans
200ml crème fraiche
300g mayonnaise
salt and pepper
paprika

Method

Pre-heat the oven to 190°C (gas mark 5)

Finely chop the parmesan in a food processor and place in an oven dish. Purée the onion, garlic, one tin of artichokes and half the tin of beans and add to the dish.

Roughly chop in the remaining artichokes and beans. Stir in the mayonnaise and crème fraiche, season and sprinkle a generous amount of paprika over the top.

Bake in the oven for 45 minutes and serve with toasted pitta bread.

Scrummy Tips

REPLACE THE MIXED BEANS FOR EITHER CHICK PEAS OR LENTILS FOR AN ALTERNATIVE.

TO PREPARE THE PITTA, CUT THE BREAD INTO CHUNKS AND BAKE ON A ROASTING TRAY WITH A SPLATTERING OF OLIVE OIL.

ALCOLM PATTISON
& FAMILY

ESH FRUIT & FLOW

Website: www.fruit2go.co.uk
Email: sales@fruit2u.karoo.co.uk

Roasted Red Pepper with Goats Cheese

Ingredients

2 red peppers
200g preserved cherry
tomatoes or sundried tomatoes
100g goats cheese
runny honey
pine nuts
olive oil
salt and pepper

Serves 4

Pre-heat the oven to 190°C (gas mark 5)

Cut the peppers in half, lengthways, and scoop out the insides. Place in an oven dish, cut side up, and fill equally with the drained tomatoes. Season and sprinkle a little olive oil over before placing in the oven for 20 minutes.

Remove the dish from the oven and divide the goats cheese into 4, placing a piece on top of each pepper. Drizzle a little honey over each and throw a few pine nuts over the top. Put back in the oven for another 10 minutes.

Scrummy Tips

A GORGEOUS STARTER OR SUBSTANTIAL LUNCHTIME MEAL SIMPLY SERVED WITH A DRESSED GREEN SALAD.

SWAP THE TOMATOES FOR A READY-MADE COUSCOUS OR TABOULEH BUT ADD THESE ALONG WITH THE GOATS CHEESE FOR THE LAST 10 MINUTES.

Camembert Parcels

Ingredients

250g packet of ready-made filo
pastry
250g french camembert
220g caramelised red onion
chutney
pine nuts or hazelnuts, toasted
40g butter, melted
salt and pepper

Serves 4

Pre-heat the oven to 190°C (gas mark 5)

Take 2 sheets of filo pastry per parcel and cut into 2
halves.

Place a sheet of pastry on a board and brush some melted
butter all over, layering another sheet over it at a different
angle and brushing it with butter. Repeat the process two
more times, layering the sheets at different angles.

Spoon a generous dollop of chutney into the centre of the
pastry, placing a $1/4$ of the camembert on top. Sprinkle a
few of the nuts over, add a pinch of salt and pepper and
then wrap up the parcel. Pinch the filo pastry at the top to
help close and secure the parcel.

Brush the parcel with butter, wrap a little greaseproof
paper around the top leaves to stop it burning and place
on a baking sheet or in an oven dish. Bake for 30 minutes
and serve straight from the oven with a simple salad.

Scrummy Tips

ADD FRESH OR DRIED
CRANBERRIES FOR A
MORE SEASONAL TOUCH.
FOR A STRONGER TASTE,
TRY A BLUE CHEESE WITH
SLICES OF RIPE PEAR AND
WALNUTS.

THIS DISH MAKES A GREAT
STARTER FOR SUPPER OR
A SUBSTANTIAL LUNCH.

Winter Steak Salad

Ingredients

1 shallot, sliced
1 lemon grass
1 square inch ginger, peeled
1 red chilli, de-seeded
1 lemon
150ml water
2 teaspoons sugar
100ml white wine vinegar
3 tablespoons olive oil
250g fillet steak
80g sugar
80g walnuts, shelled
25g butter
1 teaspoon sugar
2 pears
125g goats cheese
2 teaspoons runny honey
50g caperberries
1 tablespoon balsamic glaze
baby spinach
radicchio

Serves 4

Prepare the steak 24 hours ahead to infuse the flavours!
Cut the steak into 3 or 4 chunks and place in a bowl. Add the zest and juice of the lemon. Finely chop the shallot, lemon grass, ginger, chilli, water, 2 teaspoons of sugar, vinegar and oil in a food processor and pour over the steak. Cover and chill.

The following day, pre-heat the oven to 190°C (gas mark 5). In a frying pan, even out the 80g sugar and slowly heat until it has caramelised. The consistency should be runny and gooey. Carefully roll the walnuts in the sugar and then place individually on some greaseproof paper to set.

Core the pears and slice each into eight. Put them in an oven dish along with the butter and the teaspoon of sugar and roast for half an hour until slightly brown and soft. Leave to cool.

On your platter, or individual plates, layer some of the spinach and radicchio. Sprinkle over the caperberries and add the crumbled goats cheese. Drizzle the honey over the goats cheese to soften it.

Prepare the steak, last minute, by heating a frying pan and literally searing the steak for 30 seconds each side, turning until the steak has browned on all sides. Lift out of the pan and slice thinly. It will be lovely and red in the centre and brown on the outside.

Add the meat to the salad along with the cooked pears and crunchy walnuts. Drizzle with the balsamic glaze and it's ready to serve. The flavours are amazing!

Chocolate Brownies

Ingredients

250g unsalted butter
200g plain chocolate (at least 70% cocoa solids)
4 large free-range eggs, beaten
80g cocoa powder
65g plain flour
1 teaspoon baking powder
360g soft dark brown sugar

Method

Pre-heat the oven to 180°C (gas mark 4)

Line a 25cm square baking tin with greaseproof paper and grease.

Melt the chocolate and butter over a pan of simmering water, in a bowl. Mix in a separate bowl the cocoa powder, flour, baking powder and sugar then add the melted chocolate and stir well, slowly adding the beaten egg until you have a lovely glossy mixture.

Pour into the tin and bake in the oven for 25 minutes. The top should be slightly hard and crispy but the middle will be soft and gooey! Cool and then place in the fridge to help it set. It will be easier to cut when cold.

When ready, cut into squares and see how long it is before you set to and make it again!

Scrummy Tips

SERVE WARM, STRAIGHT FROM THE OVEN, FOR AN IRRESISTIBLE DESSERT WITH A DOLLOP OF CREAM OR CREME FRAICHE - CHOCOLATE HEAVEN!
ADD UP TO 100G OF CHOPPED NUTS, CHERRIES OR DRIED FRUIT TO THE MIXTURE BEFORE BAKING FOR EVEN MORE OF TREAT!

Caramelised Oranges

Ingredients

600g clementines or oranges
300ml water
250g golden caster sugar
1 lemon
1 cinnamon stick

Serves 6

Peel the oranges and layer in a dish or bowl. Whole clementines or slices of orange will do the same trick. Put half the orange peel in a food processor and chop finely. Discard the remaining peel.

Using the chopped orange peel to infuse flavour, boil it in a saucepan along with the water, sugar, lemon zest and lemon juice. Throw in the cinnamon stick and simmer for 15 minutes, until the sugar has dissolved and the water has caramelised slightly.

Leave to cool and then pour over the oranges, discarding the cinnamon stick. Chill in the fridge for at least 3 hours and serve either on their own or with cream.

Scrummy Tips

THIS MAKES A GREAT REFRESHING PUDDING TO A HEAVY CHRISTMAS DINNER!

THE FRUIT IS REFRESHING YET THE SAUCE HAS ALL THOSE SUGARY TREATS

Ginger and Orange Christmas Log

Ingredients

300g ginger biscuits
100ml ginger ale
1 orange
1 stem ginger
250ml double cream
2 tablespoons caster sugar
1 chocolate flake

Serves 4

Pour the ginger ale into a bowl along with the juice and zest of the orange. Slice the stem ginger into little pieces and add to the liquid.

You have to be quick with this bit! With your platter at the ready, soak the ginger biscuits for about 30 seconds in the bowl and then carefully lift them out and re-stack them in a line on your platter. Pour over the leftover juices (now thicker) and let the biscuits soak up the mixture for at least half an hour in the fridge.

When ready to serve, quickly whip up the cream and sugar with an electric whisk and spread over the log. Using a knife, make bark-like representations and finish off with the crumbled chocolate flake or grated chocolate. Maybe even a sprig of holly too?

Mincemeat and Syrup Sponge Pudding

Ingredients

100g margarine
100g caster sugar
2 medium free-range eggs
225g self-raising flour
2 tablespoons milk
2 tablespoons golden syrup
2 tablespoons good quality mincemeat

Serves 4

Grease a 1.2 litre (2 pint) pudding basin. Spoon in the syrup and mincemeat.

Blend and cream the margarine, sugar and eggs with a little of the flour.

Fold in the remaining flour with the milk and pour on top of the syrup and mincemeat.

Cover with greaseproof paper or tin foil, folding and pleating the edges to secure. Steam in a pan of boiling water for 1 1/2 hours. Serve with custard or cream.

Scrummy Tips

REPLACE THE SYRUP AND MINCEMEAT WITH JAM FOR A JAM SPONGE PUDDING. ALTERNATIVELY, ADD A LITTLE GROUND GINGER WITH THE FLOUR AND MIX IN SOME CHOPPED STEM GINGER WITH THE SYRUP TOPPING FOR A LOVELY GINGER SPONGE.